W9-BIF-017

Sonia Gallico

guide to the **FORA**
and the **COLISEUM**

with a section about the Domus Aurea

ATS ITALIA EDITRICE

INTRODUCTION

The very ancient legend of the birth of Rome (the date of the mythic foundation goes back to 21st April 754 or 753), links the origins of the town to the famous destruction of Troy on the coasts of Asia Minor, by the Greeks. The hero Aeneas, son of the goddess Venus, is said to have fled with his father Anchises and his son Ascanius. After a long wandering, they landed on Latium coasts where Aeneas founded the town of Lavinium. One of his descendents, Rhea Silvia, Vest's priestess, was then loved by the god Mars. They had twins, Romulus and Remus, who were abandoned, while still infants, in the river Tiber. Found by a farmer, they were nursed in a cave and fed by a she-wolf. Once adults, they decided to found a town, marking a square furrow on the Palatine Hill; the one who saw more birds flying in the sky would give the name to the town. Romulus won, as he saw twice as many birds as his brother. So he decided to name the new town - Rome; but Remus, as an insult, stepped over the furrow around the area on which the new town was to be built – thus Romulus killed him to take revenge. The town was then ruled by the famous seven kings: Romulus, Numa Pompilius, Tullus Hostilius, Ancus Marcius, Tarquin the Elder, Servius Tullius, Tarquin the Proud – the last three were of Etruscan origin. In 509 BC the Monarchy fell and the Republic was established.

The archaeological finds confirm the tradition. The experts agree to consider the Palatine Hill the first settlement of Rome. Here, since 1950 researchers have revealed traces of primitive settlings, dating back to the 9th – 8th centuries BC. They were opening holes in the rocks, with the poles of the huts driven in, surrounded by furrows for rain drainage. But other settlements were probably on the surrounding hills. Unfortunately, at present we have no traces of them . Towards the 8th c. BC, a market was founded on the left bank of the river, near the Tiber Island and the river port - perhaps situated behind the building of the current Registry Office – it was an exchanging place outside the built-up area, and for this reason it was called foro (from foras = outside), that is the so-called Forum Boarium. During the 7th and 6th centuries, under the Etruscan hegemony, Rome had great development. It was then that a little farther north, the Forum Holitorium had its origin, extending from the Theatre of Marcellus and Via della Consolazione. In that period, on the Capitoline Hill, a great temple was built, dedicated to three divinities, who were often worshipped together in the Latin world (Jupiter, Minerva and Juno) – some traces can still be seen above all inside the Palazzo Caffarelli. The area situated to the east, later on the site of the Roman Forum, was used as a burial ground. The marshy valley was drained at the end of the 6th c. with the building of the Great Sewer – the "Cloaca Maxima"; this area became the very heart of the Republican and Imperial Rome.

THE REPUBLICAN AGE During the first years of the Republic, the dominion of Rome extended northwards to Veii and southwards to Capua, so that the town kept on expanding. In the middle of the 5th c. there was a sudden stop in the building development because of the struggles between the patricians and the plebeians. In the III and II centuries BC the expansion wars in the Mediterranean Sea (Taranto was conquered in 272 and Carthage destroyed in 146) did not interfere with the revival of the urban growth. Unfortunately we have few traces of the buildings dating back to this period, because the Romans used to rebuild the monuments of the past, throughout the centuries leaving only the dedication, in contrast with the modern trend to preservation.
During the II century BC, the Roman Forum became the main square in Rome, adorned with temples and basilicas.

At the beginning of the I century BC the Tabularium was built (then incorporated into the Senatorium Palace) and the temples of the Fortuna Virilis and Vesta (both in the Forum Boarium) were then erected.

With Julius Caesar, the great leader conqueror of Gaul, Rome acquired new splendour. He built another square, next to the traditional forum, just to enlarge the centre, which had become too small for the late-Republican Rome. The theatre of Marcellus dates from this period of the century.

The urban politics of Augustus was even greater and more ambitious than Caesar's, as it went beyond the mere area of the Forum. He built new places, such as one more Forum with a temple that was even grander than Caesar's temple, public baths dedicated to Agrippa, an Amphitheatre and public Libraries. Campus Martius was even enlarged and a monumental imposing tomb was built for the Emperor, his family and his successors, who all carried out the ideals to construct greater buildings. Nero (54-68 AD), after the fire of 64 AD which destroyed a great part of the town, started to construct new town buildings. A new "Town Planning Scheme" was carried out with straight and larger roads, a market - the so-called Macellum Magnum - was built at the Celian Hill and the Neronian Baths sprung up at Campus Martius. On the Esquiline, Oppian and Palatine Hills, the new magnificent residence of the Emperor - the Domus Aurea - was erected, only a part of the Pavilion on the Oppian Hill has been recently restored and opened to the public.

The Flavian Age (Vespasian 69-79; Titus 78-81; Domitian 81-96) was also characterised by two great fires, one in 69 AD on the Capitoline Hill, and the other in 80 AD on the Capitoline and in Campus Martius. The Flavian Amphitheatre dates from this period, begun by Vespasian and completed by his son Titus in 80 AD. According to the tradition, it was inaugurated with spectacular shows which lasted 100 days, during which 500 wild animals and many gladiators died. Nerva (96-98) built his own forum, beside that of Augustus, while the Emperor Trajan built the greatest group of squares, basilicas and markets that Rome had ever seen. All these works are attributed to Apollodorus of Damascus. Unfortunately part of this majestic group of the "Imperial Fora" was destroyed with the building of Via dei

4

Fori Imperiali, inaugurated during the Fascist Era in 1932. It links Piazza Venezia and the Coliseum towards the sea. The road split the ancient town complex into two parts, made of adjoining and perpendicular squares. It has been one of the worst urban errors in our contemporary history. For a long time experts have been consulting about the chance to cancel this large artery, so as to connect again, the Imperial with the Republican Forum.

Other Roman Emperors left important traces in Rome - Hadrian (117-138) who erected the temple of Venus (opposite the Coliseum) and completely restored the Pantheon and then Caracalla (211-217) with his famous Baths. But the deep crisis of the Empire had already begun, in fact Aurelian (270-275) surrounded the town with mighty walls, which were to be a lasting mark during the Middle Ages and the Renaissance, intact up until now. With Diocletian (284-305) there was a certain growth of the building activities; the biggest baths ever seen were built, (today situated near Termini Station). The Roman building technique reached its pinnacle. This politics was followed by Maxentius (306-312), who built the famous basilica and by Constantine (306-337) who gave Rome great and various monuments.

THE PALEOCHRISTIAN AND THE MIDDLE AGES

Emperor Constantine issued the important Edict of Milan in 313: the Catholic religion, already established in the Empire, could be practised, after all the previous and numerous persecutions. Several new buildings for the new cult were built, the so-called "basilicas". Some of them stand within the walls, as Santa Maria Maggiore, San Giovanni and Santa Sabina; others are outside, as St Peter's, San Paolo fuori le Mura and San Lorenzo. Almost all of them were built with columns and precious marbles taken from buildings in ruin. Several proclamations were edited during the 4th and 5th c. to invite the population not to destroy the great glories of a still present past. But already in 330 the capital of the Empire was moved from Rome to Constantinople and, at the end of the 4th - beginning of the 5th c., Milan and then Ravenna (in 402) became the seats of the Western Roman Empire. For almost two centuries the magnificent Byzantine art flourished in Ravenna. After the invasion of the Visigots in 410 and Vandals in 455, Rome began to decline as it was partly abandoned - only at the beginning of the new millennium the city flourished again.

FORUM BOARIUM AND FORUM HOLITORIUM

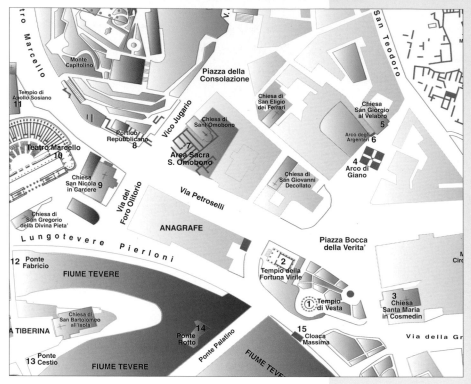

The earliest public places of archaic Rome were founded in the area situated among the left bank of the river Tiber, the churches of Santa Maria in Cosmedin, San Giorgio in Velabro and the theatre of Marcellus. In fact, from the 8th century BC on, the populations living on the surrounding hills traded in the plain near the Tiber; many remains bear witness of that age.

Here rose the Forum Boarium - its name (perhaps from bos, bovis = bull) lets us suppose it was a cattle market. It has been located in the square faced by Santa Maria in Cosmedin.

In the 6th century BC, a little farther north, the Forum Holitorium (perhaps its name comes from oleum = oil) a vegetable market was founded, placed by archeologists near San Nicola in Carcere. In these places various temples were erected; today we have just two of them, dating from the II and the I centuries BC: the so-called temple of Vesta and that devoted to the god Portumnos.

The city plan, as you see it nowadays, was designed in 1920-30 by the architect Antonio Muñoz, who destroyed a medieval quarter, isolating the ancient buildings.

TEMPLE OF VESTA

It dates back to the Republican Age (II-I centuries BC). Made of marble from Mount Pentelico, near Athens, it has the same shape of a temple in Delphi (Greece), dedicated to the goddess Athena. Slightly raised, it is made up of a round cella and a circular portico, with 20 Corinthian columns. Probably dedicated to the god Hercules, it is usually called Temple of Vesta, from the name of the divinity protectress of hearth and home and also of the city of Rome. In fact, it is similar to another situated in the Roman Forum, dedicated to the goddess Vesta, too. It became a Christian church – Santa Maria del Sole - during the Middle Ages, but it was restored to its original forms in the '20s. Inside you will find a fresco referring to the Roman school of art, dating back to the end of the 15th century and representing the recently restored "Virgin Mary and her Son".

Triton Fountain

The Triton Fountain (1717) is situated nearby, commissioned by Pope Clement XI (1720-21); his heraldic coat-of-arms with three mounts and an eight-pointed star is located at the base of the pipe where water comes out from.

Incorrectly called temple of "Fortuna Virilis", it was more probably dedicated to Portumnos, the protector of the harbour activities along the river. It is one of the most ancient temples in Rome,
dating back, in the form it has today, to the I century BC. Traces
still remain, dating from the 5th century, although it was restored
during the III century BC. It has the typical form of the Roman
temples: through terrace stairs you enter a high podium where
you will find the cella, preceded by an open pronaos (=atrium).
The Ionic frontal columns are in travertine, while the semicolumns are tufa made, like the external walls; the bases, the capitals
and the top parts are in travertine. The whole was refined with
stucco – evident traces can still be seen on the columns.
The temple is one of the best preserved as, in the 9th century, or
even before, it was transformed into a Christian church, dedicated to Santa Maria Egiziaca. Witnesses of this change may be
seen on the wide rectangular windows opened on the long side
wall, facing the Tiber. The temple was studied a lot during the
Renaissance, also by important artists such as Serlio, Palladio and
Piranesi; then Pope Pius V (1566-72) donated the temple of
Fortuna Virilis to the Armenian community in Rome. Its restoration, begun in the 19th century, was completed in 1925, thanks to
the architect Antonio Muñoz, who introduced the so-called "simplified forms" – that is without details, so as to distinguish easily
the "ancient" from the "new" – look at the mouldings of the
architrave on the columns .

SANTA MARIA IN COSMEDIN

It was built in different phases on Roman pre-existing sites. In the 6th century AD, a group of people, probably from Constantinople, erected a small one-nave building with an apse at the far end which had to gather a diaconiae. In Costantinople stood a church with the same dedication (the Greek word "Cosmedin" means "the beautiful and the decorated church"). Pope Hadrian I (772-795) restored the church - the nave was flanked by two side aisles ending with two smaller apses. Early in the 12th century Calist II (119-124) restored the church, above all in the atrium- he added the bell tower, which lightens towards the top, as always during the Romanic age.

Altered during the 17th and 18th centuries, it was restored to its probable "Romanic" form since 1890.

The external typical prothyrum, supported on different columns, was built before, in the 8th century, and it is considered the base of the restoration of the following centuries. In the atrium you will find the famous Bocca della Verità (Mouth of Truth), a small Roman tomb, around which, during the Middle Ages, flourished a legend: the mouth would snap shut on the hand

Bocca della Verità

of a thief who lied before the court, pleading not guilty.

Inside, the nave and the side aisles were separated by alternate pillars and three columns (all deriving from ancient monuments with late Corinthian capitals), lit by small windows. The stone floor has insets with geometric patterns and it dates back to the 12th century, while the ceiling is modern .The transenna of the schola cantorum (place reserved to the choral group) is of the 12th century; the tabernacle (cyborium) over the altar and the choir date from the 13th century.

In the right chapel is situated the famous "Virgin Mary and her Son", here since 1898; before it was in the apse of the church. Some historians attribute it to Cimabue (13th century), others date it to the 5th century.

An 8th-century AD mosaic is situated in the right-hand side room. The controfaçade incorporates some columns from spolia.

Arch the Janus, detail

Arch of Janus

The name derives from ianus (a covered passage) and the building dates back to the beginning of the 4th century AD. It was probably commissioned by Constantine (306-337) or by his son Costanzo II (337-340), and it presents four arcades held up by four massive pillars, on which you will see some niches, once used for statues. A cross vault covers the interior.

Incorporated in a medieval fortress, it was restored to its original form in the '20s and '30s, when all the area was refurbished.

The church of San Giorgio in Velabro belongs to an unusual, but nonetheless suggestive Rome, made of small churches and hidden views; it is surely worth visiting. Situated in an area hollowed out by the Velabrum, an ancient stream which flowed into the Tiber after having crossed the Forum, this is one of the most ancient churches in the city. Built at the end of the 7th century, the Church was enlarged in 830 by Pope Gregory IV (827-844) , who added the two aisles, so giving it the existing structure. The 13th century portico includes pre-existing remains; the bell tower, lighting towards the top, typically Romanic in style, dates from the 13th century. The internal columns made with material taken from ancient buildings, are all unique. Worth noting is the raising of the altar, a stylistic trend which will be used in the Romanic period. The left-side wall is oblique and asymmetric, if compared to the right-side one, because it was erected on an existing structure. During the Middle Ages, they used to build quickly, sometimes re-employing ancient material, without taking care of the rules of symmetry and cohesion among the various parts. The cyborium (over the altar) dates from the end of the 12th c. The fresco situated on the back-ground of the apse and restored seve-ral times, is attributed to Cavallini (13th century) or even to Giotto (beginning of the 14th century). The church, abandoned during the 16th c., was then restored in 1610 with Baroque decorations; then in the 18th century it became a storehouse for oil and wine. In 1824 the architect Giuseppe Valadier planned a restoration of the church, but it remained just a plan. In 1926 the architect Antonio Muñoz took the building to its probable "primitive" origin with a radical intervention. In July 1993, a bomb attack destroyed the right-front side of the portico and damaged the interior, also. The Sovrintendenza ai Beni Architettonici e Storici of Rome restored the church to the structure it had been like before the explosion.

Built in 204 by money-changing Bankers (argentarii) and bull merchants (negoziantes boarii), in honour of the Emperor Septimius Severus, it was the gateway to the commercial area.

ARCH OF THE ARGENTARI

In the '30s, opposite the church of St Omobono, two archaic temples were excavated - they probably refer back to the reign of king Servius Tullius (6th century BC). They are probably the temples of Fortuna and Magna Mater (a divinity protector of the fertility of the Earth, also called Cibele) with front altars. Crossing Via del Vico Jugario, you can see the remains of the late Republican portico with Tuscan columns (I century BC).

ARCHEOLOGICAL SITE OF SAINT OMOBONO

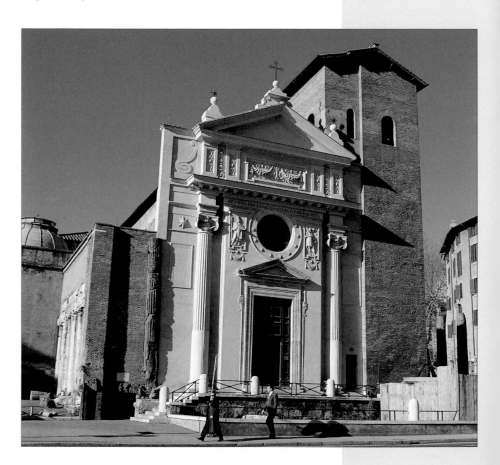

On the opposite side of Via Luigi Petroselli, former Via del Teatro di Marcello, then Via del Mare, stands the church of San Nicola in Carcere. According to the tradition, the name refers to the presence here of a prison; the walls incorporate the remains of

SAN NICOLA IN CARCERE

San Nicola in Carcere, Roman columns

columns of three Roman temples, the foundations of which are still visible. It probably dates from the 8th century, but it was built in the 12th century and restored in the Renaissance. The façade was designed by Giacomo della Porta in 1599. It presents a giant Ionic order which frames the portal and the round window; over it, you will see a projecting entablature adorned with garland and festoon patterns - the tympanum lies on it. The medieval tower has been recently restored.

THEATRE OF MARCELLUS The theatre was begun by Julius Caesar in 46 BC and, after his death in 44 BC, it was completed by Augustus. In 22 BC, Augustus dedicated it to Marcus Claudius Marcellus, his sister Octavia's son, predestined to succeed him, but died at only 19.

It was inaugurated in 21 BC or, according to some historians in 13 BC, with the killing of 600 wild animals. We do not know the name of the architect, even if the theatre follows the "rules" of the famous ancient theoretician Vitruvius Pollio. The semi-circular theatre presents an external travertine prospect, 32 m high. It was characterized by framed arcades, introduced in an original way, in the architectonic orders - Doric, Ionic, Corinthian one over the other (no traces are left of the last order). This type of architecture, here used for

Theatre of Marcellus, detail of the Renaissance windows

the first time, served as a typical model for the façades of Roman theatres and amphitheatres and for the Coliseum itself. The cavea, seating about 15000 spectators, had a 130m diameter, while the orchestra

Theatre of Marcellus, detail of the Doric order

was 37 m wide; these parts no longer exist. We know that the scene, destroyed in 64 AD by a great fire, was rebuilt by Vespasian (69-79) and Alexander Severus (222-235).

The Theatre was used in its proper functions, till the second half of the 4th century (about 370). It was then abandoned and, in the 12th century it was converted into a famous fortress, then enlarged by the Savelli family in the 13th and 14th centuries. During the Renaissance, the theatre was still admired by architects who used, in their palaces, the three superimposed orders; in 1523-27 it was "restored" by Baldassarre Peruzzi, a refined artist from Siena, who bricked up the top storey, opening the still visible elegant windows. In the 18th century the palace passed to the Orsini family; during the 19th century many houses and shops were built inside it. From 1926 to 1932 the theatre was restored and cleared of the workshops which were in the lower storey. Then it was decided to build a buttress in order to consolidate the palace. The restoration by Baldassarre Peruzzi is still standing and leaves visible traces of the passing of time.

TEMPLE OF APOLLO SOSIANUS

In 1940, on the right of the theatre of Marcellus, three columns belonging to the so-called Temple of Apollo Sosianus were re-erected and reassembled spectacularly together with the entablature. The name "Apollo Sosianus" derives from the consul Caius Sosius, who built the temple in 34 BC. It is estimated it was 29,20 m. high. The travertine columns were refined with stuccoes. The sculptures on the tympanum (5th century BC), were brought to Rome at the end of the I century BC from the Greek region of Eubea, as spoils of war. These statues have been recently reassembled in the former Power Station Montemartini, now converted into a Museum. In the same area, there was also the Temple of Bellona devoted to that eastern divinity, no longer existing. The medieval buildings in the back were restored during the first decades of our century and today seat the council offices. On the back of the Theatre, the remains of the Portico of Octavia may be admired.

ROMAN FORUM

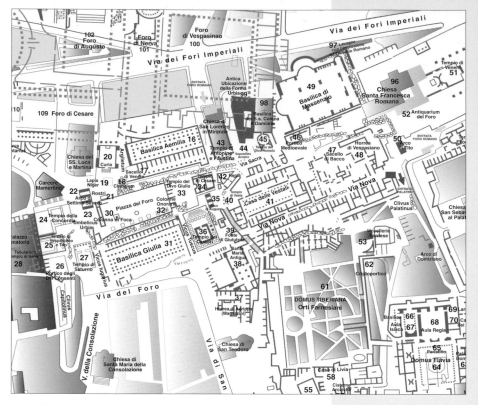

I n origin (9th-7th centuries BC), the Roman Forum was an isolated burial ground, used by a community who developed near the Tiber (see Forum Boarium and Holitorium). The site of the forum (from Latin foras = out of the town centre) was drained towards the 600 BC, thanks to the building of a big sewer (Cloaca Maxima), which carried the waters from the surrounding hills to the Tiber.

During the Republican Age (6th century BC) it became the most important square, because it was the commercial and political centre of Rome. In the Imperial period, (since the I century AD) it maintained its functions and other public areas were built.

It is rectangular in shape, linked to the Palatine and the Capitoline Hills through the Via Sacra. It was continually being transformed. Politicians and emperors contributed to its continuous enrichment, building new places and restoring buildings and monuments. They date from different ages, only through the flowing of time have they reached an homogeneous aspect, hiding the differences behind the patina of the centuries.

Entrance to the Fora from the Coliseum

From Via dei Fori Imperiali, after a short descent, you will be directly on the Via Sacra, the road which linked the Palatine to the Capitoline, where the most important temple in the city stood. It was dedicated to Jupiter Capitolinus. During the Kings' time, the road was paved for the first time; what we see now, made of basalt slabs, dates back to Augustus' age, the first Emperor of Rome (27 BC - 14 AD). Along the Via Sacra, victorious armies, coming back from military campaigns, rode in triumphant processions, taking back with them war trophies and chained prisoners, reduced to slavery. The final part of the Via Sacra has been recently brought to light and it is visible from the Belvedere on the Capitoline. From the right-hand side, you will reach all the area at the foot of the Capitoline Hill.

VIA SACRA

BASILICA AEMILIA

Soon on the right of the ramp, there is a slab with an inscription in capital letters dedicated to the Emperor Augustus' son, Lucius Caesar (great Julius' grandson). Behind the remains of the Basilica Aemilia, lies a rectangular building, used for civil activities, justice administration and money-changers. The entrance was on the longer side towards the forum, on which a line of tabernae (=shops) stood. The building was divided into four aisles, one of which was very wide and higher than the others. It was named after Marcus Emilius Lepidus, the magistrate who planned to build it in 179 BC. It was rebuilt at the beginning of the I century AD and restored at the beginning of the 5th century AD, after a fire probably connected to the siege of Rome, in 410 by the Goths. The present visible remains date from this phase. Outside the Basilica, you will see the traces of a round building, marked by a nameplate; it was the so-called Sacello of Venus Cloacina, a small round temple indicating the way in of the main sewer to the forum (Cloaca Maxima). Going on, towards the Capitoline, you will admire the Comitium - an area opposite the Senate, where popular assemblies were held. It was the heart of the Roman politics during the Republican Age.

Slab dedicated to Lucius Caesar

On the left-hand side of the Basilica Aemilia, opposite the forum, there is the level of a previous basilica and the structures of the Cloaca Maxima - the big sewer, already described, dug in the 6th century, during the Etruscan dominion. A discharging arch protected it from the superimposed buildings.

The majestic building of the Curia, seat of the Roman Senate, is 21 m high. It was rebuilt several times and what remains today refers to Diocletian's age (284-305 AD). Recent excavations have discovered structures dating from the end of the I century BC - these works show that the previous structure faced the Forum of Caesar which was situated behind it, in a reversed direction. Under Pope Onorius I (625-638) the Curia became a church - Saint Hadrian. Restored in the Baroque Age, it was brought back to its primitive state during the '30s.

Inside, on the two lateral podiums, sat 300 senators, elected by the population. They sat on one side or another, according to their favourable or unfavourable vote. At the far end of the Curia, there is a porphyry statue which was found in the back of the building -

Interior of the Curia

it was the place once occupied by the now lost statue of the Goddess of Victory. On both sides, there are two great carved slabs, called "Trajan's Plutei": they have an architectonic background giving an interesting image of the Roman Forum in the ancient age. The left-hand side slab represents the Emperor remitting debts to some Roman citizens and the consequent destruction of the records containing the overdue taxes. The right-hand slab shows the distribution of economic aids to assist the poor.

LAPIS NIGER   Opposite the Curia is the famous Lapis Niger (=black stone), a small square area, probably covered by black stone slabs at Caesar's time, under which, according to the tradition, the tomb of Romulus lies, the first king of Rome in the 8th century BC.

According to more realistic hypotheses, it was the place where the founder of the town was killed, suspected to have become too strong. Preserved here is the most ancient inscription in archaic Latin (with letters from left to right and on the following line, from right to left), probably dating from the Kings' age. Some parts are missing - its meaning is almost obscure and it probably indicates this sacred place and the prohibition to profane it.

Basement of the Decennalia

Not far, you will see the basement of the Decennalia, a monument which celebrates the ten- year reign of the Tetrarchy (=the division of the Empire into four parts, to rule it more easily), built by the Emperor Diocletian in 293 AD.

Beyond the Lapis Niger stands the arch of Septimius Severus (193-211). As it appears in the attic, it was erected by the Emperor in 203 to celebrate his struggles against the Parthians - a population of the present Iran. It has three arcades and it is 21 m high; the lateral reliefs illustrate war scenes with prisoners in chains and predict already the loss of proportion of the figures, typical of the late ancient period, as compared to the classical rules. Worth noting in the dedicatory text is the forth line from the top: the name of Geta, Septimius Severus' son, was obliterated by Geta's brother, Caracalla, who killed him treacherously, so as to erase his memory. However, the holes of the letters are still visible.

Beside the left fornix stands the so-called Umbelicus Urbis, a small brick building of the same period of the arch, marking the centre of the city - it dates back to the Republican age.

ARCH OF SEPTIMIUS SEVERUS

Arch of Septimius Severus, detail

THE CAPITOLINE HILL

This sacred hill hosted the most important religious buildings in the city. Facing the forum, they were the final destination of the religious cerimonies and official processions which walked down the Via Sacra. The ancient Capitoline Hill was characterised by two high points - the Arx and the Capitolium, separated by the declivity of the Asylum. The temple of Juno Moneta (=councellor) stood on the Arx , on which was later erected, the medieval church of Ara Coeli. The Capitolium was the seat of the biggest temple in the city, dedicated to the Capitoline Triad of Jupiter, Juno and Minerva, dating from the end of the 6th century BC. Some remains are still in the Palazzo dei Conservatori, in the back gardens and in the near Palazzo Caffarelli. On this side, there was also a precipice called Tarpeian Rock (Rupe Tarpea). According to the tradition, the name comes from a Roman girl –Tarpeja – who was hurled into the void by the Sabine invaders, even though she had opened the gates of the city for them. In the middle of the 16th century, the Hill was completely restored, according to the plan commissioned to Michelangelo, who decided to turn the direction of the hill, ideally linking it to St. Peter's Basilica. Today the buildings of the square are also the seat of the local authority which administers Rome (Comune di Roma). The Senatorium Palace (Palazzo Senatorio), situated in the centre, has incorporated the structures of the ancient Tabularium, still visible from the Roman Forum. The building, which was to house the tabulae of the law (=state records) was made of wide blocks of tufa (opus quadratum) and comprised two orders of arcades on pillars with Doric semi-columns on a high basement. The side towers date from the

Capitol Square

Temple of Saturn

Medieval and Renaissance ages. Below the Tabularium, from right to left, there were: 1) the temple of Concord, erected to commemorate the re-establishment (367 BC) of peace between the patricians and the plebeians; then it was rebuilt in the I century AD on former structures dating from the 4th c. BC. The only existing remain is the external wall. 2) The temple begun by Vespasian (69-79) and completed under Domitian (81-96) - it has three intact columns still. 3) The portico of the Dei Consenti (= of the gathering of the gods) has columns with splendid Corinthian capitals, dating from the end of the I century AD and rebuilt in the 4th c. AD. In the hall, bent as an obtuse angle, there were six rooms each housing a statue of divinity. 4) The Temple of Saturn with its still existing eight columns in the front portico, was built on an altar, dating back to the Kings' age. During the Roman period, it was rebuilt three times in the same place, the present one dates from the 4th c. AD. Each year, from 17th to 23rd December, the Saturnalia festivals were celebrated here and the Romans used to dress up and make jokes, while the slaves would sit at the table with their masters or even be served by them.

Temple of Vespasian

THE ROSTRA

Returning to the internal part of the forum, which was the main political area, on the left, you will find the Rostra. It was a raised platform where the orators spoke to the crowd.

Built at the end of the I century BC, the Rostra derived its name from the colossal rams (prows of the enemy ships) of the 4th century, which adorned the front part; the links are still visible on the basement wall.

COLUMN OF PHOCAS

It is the latest monument in the forum. The Eastern Emperor Phocas built it in 608 – he re-used a column of the II century and placed a statue on it. On the left, there is a fence with a fig tree, an olive tree and a vine, which remind us of an old legend: to appease the Hades gods' wrath, a knight jumped into a lake, and these three plants began then to grow. On the floor, an inscription with bronze letters (reconstructed) bears the name of Surdinus, the Roman magistrate who restored the forum after a devasting fire in 14 AD.

BASILICA JULIA

Almost symmetric to the Basilica Aemilia, it was begun by Julius Caesar in 54 BC on the site of a previous basilica, called "Sempronia". The aim was to close the southern side of the Forum. It was completed by Augustus, rebuilt after a fire in 12 AD, and then restored in 284 by Diocletian. With the same rectangular shape, it was slightly raised with four aisles and a wide central nave. On the stairs, it is still possible to

see some carved games, similar to our draughts. From the Basilica Julia, you can see what remains of seven columns reassembled in the 19th century with high basements, referring to the age of Emperor Diocletian; each column was topped by a statue.

Going left, the first building is the so-called Altar of Caesar – you will see the remains of a temple built by Augustus in 29 BC to honour his predecessor. Caesar was stabbed to death in a trap organized by Brutus and Cassius, (leaders of the conspirators) outside the Cury of Pompey, near the current Argentina Theatre. Here he was cremated on the Ides of March (15th March 44 BC). Even today, Romans and tourists still lay flowers on the monument, to honour the great politician.

ALTAR OF CAESAR

On the right, there are the remains of the temple of Castor and Pollux, or the Dioscuri, rebuilt on a pre-existing temple of the II c. AD. Today we have just three magnificent columns in Corinthian style. The monument was erected to commemorate the battle on the shores of Lake Regillus – on the Alban Hills, near Rome - (499 BC) during which the Romans, saw the divine twins, riding horses and fighting side by side. They defeated the Latins, thus starting the expansion of Latium. Under the podium, there were small rooms, probably used as offices for weights and sizes.

TEMPLE OF CASTOR AND POLLUX

Behind the temple of Castor and Pollux, towards the slope of the Palatine, there are some majestic buildings, dating from Diocletian's era (81-96). Among them you will admire a great Hall with semi-circular niches in the walls (some archaeologists define it as the Scuola Superiore founded by Augustus). Behind

SANTA MARIA ANTIQUA AND THE FOUNTAIN OF JUTURNA

Fountain of Juturna

them are situated the so-called Horrea (markets) of Agrippa, of the I c. B.C. On the walls of Diocletian, next to the Palatine, the small church of Santa Maria Antiqua was founded in the 6th century. Its aim was to show life going on in the Forum also during the early Middle Ages. Only with permission are you allowed to enter and admire some of the most ancient frescoes in Rome: an 8th century Crucifixion, in which Christ is represented in a tunic, as in the Byzantine iconography. Most likely the painting was executed by an artist of Eastern origin. Not far from the church, there is the so-called Lacus Juturnae, a spring dedicated to Juturna, an archaic Latin divinity connected with the presence of other water sources; next to this, there is the harmonic classical niche with Corinthian capitals, restored under the Emperor Trajan at the beginning of the III c. AD. Going back towards the altar of Caesar, you will note the few remains of an Arch built to commemorate the Victory of Augustus over Cleopatra, queen of Egypt. This three- arcade arch was erected in 29 BC.

TEMPLE OF VESTA Past the ruins of the arch of Augustus, on the left, you will see traces of the ancient Regia, home of the kings of the archaic era. The Regia was restored at the end of the I century B.C. On the right, you will see what remains of the Temple of Vesta, rebuilt under Septimius Severus (193-211), on a pre-existing building. It presents a circular form with Corinthian columns, and it was reassembled and restored around 1930.

On the left of the Temple of Vesta, you will find the famous house of the Vestal Virgins, the priestesses who preserved the

HOUSE OF THE VESTAL VIRGINS

sacred fire in the Temple of Vesta. The house was rebuilt during Emperor Adrian's age (117-138). The houses of these young women were built around a circular atrium, with an octagonal sort of flowerbed of the 4th c. The girls were chosen among the Roman noble families. These six girls spent 30 years of their lives as priestesses, making an absolute vow of chastity. If a vestal broke her vow, she was condemned to be walled up alive! For the first 10 years the girls were instructed, for the next 10 years they carried on their duties as priestesses and, for the last 10 years they taught the young vestal virgins.

TEMPLE OF ANTONINUS AND FAUSTINA

The temple, facing the Via Sacra, was built by the Emperor Antoninus Pius (138-161) to commemorate his wife Faustina's death in 148. The Roman Senate decided to dedicate it also to Antoninus, after his death. The splendid columns are in grey marble, with Corinthian capitals, unfortunately damaged a lot. The front of the temple is well preserved, because, in the 11th century, the church of San Lorenzo in Miranda was established on it. The frameworks of the church were taken away in 1536 and in 1602 it was converted again into a church with the same dedication, thus leaving the ancient pronaos free.

On the right of the temple, there are remains of an archaic Burial Ground. Excavations in the '50s, led by the archaeologist Giacomo Boni have revealed the remains of about 40 tombs - used for burial purposes and cremation - dating back to the 10th-7th centuries BC. This fact confirms the cemeterial use of the forum during the archaic age. Some parts of the excavations can be visited at the public Antiquarium.

Next to the archaic Necropolis, stands the so-called Temple of Romulus, probably dedicated to the Emperor Maxentius' son. It was built where, according to the tradition, the first king of Rome stopped the Sabines, a population living on the hills, near the north of the city.

It consists of a hall with a curved concave wall and a circular room; these curved lines, consolidating each other, are typical of the so-called "latter antique Baroque" style of the 4th century AD. This anticipates the 16th century architecture of Bernini and Borromini .

In the 6th century, the church of Sts Cosmas and Damian, was established in the temple.

As you travel along the Via Sacra, you will pass a small medieval portico on the left, and the remains of a Sacello dedicated to the god Bacchus on the right. Then you will see - on the left - the suggestive ruins of the Basilica of Maxentius or Constantine. This grandiose three-aisle basilica was commissioned by the Emperor Maxentius (306-12).The entrance was situated on the short wall,

BASILICA OF MAXENTIUS

Statue of Constantine, foot

Statue of Constantine, hand

Statue of Constantine, head

and not on the long one, as usually in the ancient basilicas. At the far end it had an apse. The nave was covered with a cross vault, while the aisles had barrel vaults adorned with octagonal caissons. The Emperor Constantine (306-337) completed the basilica, moving the entrance from the short to the long wall and building a new apse.

The last one housed a colossal statue - 12 m high - dedicated to the Emperor. Fragments of this monument can be seen in the courtyard of the Palazzo dei Conservatori on the Capitoline. One column of the basilica is situated in the centre of Piazza di Santa Maria Maggiore.

Unfortunately what remains of this grand building are only the barrel vaults of the aisles and the springers of the cross vaults; however you can indeed imagine the splendid halls, probably 35 m high. Here the Roman building ability reached a very important technical virtuosity. On the right, in the recently opened excavation area, there are the Horrea (warehouses) of Vespasianus and, in the corner near the arch of Titus, the remains of a private Domus.

Not far from here the Forum Antiquarium stands, housed in the medieval Monastery of Santa Francesca Romana. It is peculiar for its 14th-century harmonic cloister. A great number of archaic fragments are displayed in ancient and Spartan showcases.

ARCH OF TITUS   We suggest that you go back to the Via Sacra to admire the Arch of Titus.

It has one fornix and it was erected by Domitian (81-96), to commemorate his brother Titus' campaigns in Palestine. Titus conquered Jerusalem and brought back to Rome his treausure and a multitude of slaves, as the inscription on the attic says.

Worth noting are the inside high reliefs illustrating Titus' triumph - these valuable sculptures let us suppose that the Romans had a keen knowledge of the architectonic perspective. The composite capitals (Ionic and Corinthian styles) are here used for the first time.

In the Middle Ages, the arch was incorporated in the fortress of the Frangipanis. Like the Coliseum, it was restored in the first decades of the 19th century, at first by architect Stern and then by architect Giuseppe Valadier. They built the missing parts in "simplified" forms, using the travertine and not the marble, as was its origin. Many discussions have been held because some critics have considered this restoration "very modern", as the architects have been able to reassemble the form distinguishing the old from the new; other critics have defined it mediocre, as cheap materials have been used instead of marble. The novelist Stendhal considered this restoration "a real disaster of our modern time"!

Arch of Titus, detail

TEMPLE OF VENUS

The temple was built by Hadrian (117-138) and was restored at the beginning of the 4th century. It was one of the largest temples in ancient times. It comprises two cellae with two back-to-back apses; one of these is part of the public Antiquarium. Only some Egyptian grey marble columns are still standing. From the square facing the Coliseum and Via dei Fori Imperiali, you can admire the wall of substructio (= out of the ground foundations).

34

TIME TRANSFORMATIONS IN THE

ROMAN FORUM

The Cloaca Maxima – the Great Sewer which channelled the waters from the surrounding hills (Quirinal and Capitoline) towards the Tiber – was not upkept and consequently it clogged. The valley of the Roman Forum began to change its appearance, compared to what it was like in the 7th-8th centuries AD. It was in that period that the buildings began to be slowly covered with layers of mud and other sediments, which produced a six-metre raising in the ground level.

During the Middle Ages and the Renaissance, churches and houses were built on the ruins, so as to make people soon forget the function of the below square. The stones and the marbles of the old monuments were used in the new buildings or baked in lime kilns.

In the first half of the 16th century, enormous havoc began. Pope Leon X, in a Bull of 1526, asked the Romans not to damage the still standing buildings. However ten years later, Pope Paul III sanctioned the excavation in the Forum, in order to take the marble which served for the new St. Peter's basilica. Even during the 17th century, several Roman palaces were built with stones taken from the Forum and the Coliseum.

Only at the end of the 18th century, during a Neoclassical rediscovery of the ancient Roman civilization, the first excavations were effected in the so-called "Campo Vaccino" (a field for pastures and cows), so well illustrated in the etchings by Piranesi.

Important excavations were carried on in the short period of the French occupation (1809-14). Then, from 1827, they continued under the direction of archaeologists Carlo Fea and Antonio Nibby.

Soon after the Unity of Italy from 1870 to 1886, the renowned archaeologist Rodolfo Lanciani carried out other excavations. During the first years of the 20th century Giacomo Boni led the excavation works which brought to light the Lapis Niger, a very ancient stone dating back to the Republican or even the Kings' era. The stone pointed to the most sacred place in the city, probably linked to Romulus' death.

THE PALATINE

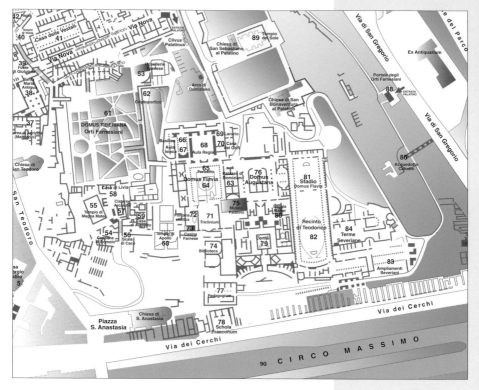

The name "Palatine" probably derives from palatium = palace. Together with the Capitoline, the Palatine is the most important hill in ancient Rome –here, in fact, the city was born, according to the sources. At the beginning, it was formed by three peaks, the Germalus – facing the Capitoline, the Palatium towards the Circus Maximus and the Velia towards the Coliseum. The Palatine was inhabited since the prehistoric age. Its fame is linked to Romulus, the legendary first king of Rome who, according to the tradition, was suckled in a cave. It was probably situated near the Velabrum or the Circus Maximus and Romulus marked out the enclosures of the city in the 8th century. During the last two centuries of the Republic, important temples were constructed – the Magna Mater and Apollo. Important politicians, such as Cicero, Hortensius, Agrippa and Marcus Antonius lived here. Since Augustus (27 BC- 14 AD), the Palatine became a residential area for patrician families and for emperors , such as Tiberius (14-37), Caligula (37-41), Claudius (41-54) and Nero (54-68). After the fire of 64, Nero enlarged his residence also on the Oppian, Esquilin and Celian Hills. Domitian (81-96) and

Nymphaeum and Farnesian Aviaries

38

finally Septimius Severus (193-211) were the last to reside on the Palatine. Enormous and majestic palaces were erected on the Palatine and , even today, it is extremely complex and difficult to understand the stratifications.

After the emperor Elagabalus (218-222), who built the terrace facing the Coliseum, the Palatine began to be abandoned. Other residences were chosen and Diocletian (284-305) built his palace at Spalato, Constantine (306-336) moved the imperial capital from Rome to Byzantium (Constantinople), thus restoring completely that town. The Palatine Hill was then chosen as residence by the barbarian kings Odoacre and Teodoricus (5th - 6th century). Ravenna became the capital of the Western Roman Empire in 402, then a more rapid and marked decay began. During the Middle Ages, the churches of Santa Maria Antiqua and San Sebastiano were erected nearby. Some convents were built on pre-existing ruins. The Frangipani family occupied it in the 11th and 12th centuries, and during the Renaissance, the Palatine was used as a cave of marble. At the end of the 16th century, the Farnese family built a majestic villa with marvellous terraced gardens, called Farnesian Horts. Today we have just some remains on the side facing the forum. Among the remains you will see the so-called "Rain Nymphaeum", the aviaries without their ancient roofs while the entrance portal was moved to Via San Gregorio. The first archaeological excavations which revealed the original Roman settlements, began in the first years of the 18th century. They continued throughout the 19th century, particularly, after the Unity of Italy in 1870. Important excavations were carried on in the 1950s, when the so-called "Romulus'Huts" were uncovered. This fact seems to confirm the legend of the founding of the city.

Archaic well

ROMULUS' HUTS

To follow a quite chronological itinerary in your visit to the Palatine, we suggest that you start from the so-called Romulus' Huts. These are the remains, discovered in 1948, of three huts dating from the 8th century BC, which confirm the presence of a village on this hill in the archaic age. The remains, protected by coverings, consist in holes dug in the tufa. They were fixed wooden stakes which held the walls probably made of earth, and small rain drainage canals which surrounded the small buildings.

No traces have been found of the Lupercale cave where, according to the legend, Romulus and Remus were brought up. It was probably situated on the south-western slope of the Palatine.

Beside Romulus'Huts, you will find the remains of the Temple of Cybele, a goddess from Asia Minor - protectress of fertility. Her cult was brought to Rome during the II Punic War, she was also called Magna Mater. According to the tradition, a ship sailing from Asia Minor to Rome, carried a black stone with the image of the goddess. The temple, standing on a basement, with a cella and six front columns, was completed in 191 BC and rebuilt several times, the last one under Augustus in 3 AD. In the cella, a statue may be found, now well preserved in the Palatine Museum.

TEMPLE OF CYBELE

A bit farther on, there are the so-called Stairs of Cacus, which brought to the Lupercale, according to the tradition. Cacus, Volcano's son, used to pass here to plunder in the below Forum Boarium; he was then killed by Hercules.

STAIRS OF CACUS

Some excavations have discovered two ancient cisterns of the 6th century BC, once buried by later buildings. They were dug in the ground and covered with tufa blocks.

ARCHAIC CISTERNS

The so-called House of Augustus, in the south-western sector, was perhaps the residence of the Emperor. According to the sources, it was originally modest, then it was enlarged during his reign (27 BC – 14 AD), and after the fire of 3 AD. It has a number of rooms surrounding a peristyle, with precious fresco decorations of the second Style of Roman painting. They are a simulation of architectonic patterns with flower and fruit festoons.

HOUSE OF AUGUSTUS

According to the historical sources, the Temple of Apollo was inaugurated in 28 BC. It had golden doors decorated with ivory, yellow marble and vivid coloured frescoes. Some fragments of those frescoes can be admired in the Palatine Museum.

TEMPLE OF APOLLO

HOUSE OF LIVIA

The House of Livia is of great interest. It consists of three small rooms on a lower level.

Frescoes representing naturalistic images have been taken off the walls so as to protect them from humidity.

The house is named after – Iulia Aug(usta) – a few letters engraved in a pipe situated in the central room.

Thus the owner of the house was supposed to be Augustus' wife, who might have lived in a wing of the Palace. The building was made up of parts of previous constructions.

Going towards the Roman Forum, you will admire what remains of Tiberius' residence (14-37), the Domus Tiberiana. It was enlarged by Caligula (37-41) and Nero (54-37) but only the walls of substructio are still standing (= out of the ground foundations). Imagine a majestic palace, no longer existing, erected on the Palatine, facing the Forum. In the second half of the 16th century, Cardinal Alessandro Farnese decided to build this sumptuous residence on its ruins, commissioning it to the architect Vignola. The visible gardens were restored during the middle of the last century. Some archaeologists suppose that the Domus Tiberiana was part of the majestic Domus Aurea, renowned residence of Nero. According to the sources, Nero extended it from the Palatine to the Oppian Hill and probably to the Esquilin (the place where Santa Maria Maggiore stands today). The suggestive cryptoporticus is a long barrel-vaulted portico which linked the various wings of the residence.

DOMUS TIBERIANA

Domus Flavia, Octagonal Fountain

PALACE OF DOMITIAN: DOMUS FLAVIA, DOMUS AUGUSTANA AND THE STADIUM

The imposing residence of the Emperor Domitian (81-96) stood in the middle of the Palatine Hill. It had filled the rather deep depression between the Germalus and Palatium Hills. The palace was divided into Domus Flavia (public area) and Domus Augustana (private area) which had some courtyards, one of which had an octagonal fountain, most of it rebuilt, and another one had a mixed linear pod. The elliptical nymphaeum is splendid, too, with its niches, once decorated with statues. Emperor Domitian built the stadium also, 160 m long and 50 m wide – the remains of the semicircular tribune are still preserved on the external side. The traces of the oval wall represent what remains of an enclosure wanted by the Emperor Theodoric (beginning of the 6th century).

On the right of the Palace of Domitian, looking towards the Circus Maximus, you will see the buildings of Pedagogium, probably a school for imperial servants and the Schola Praeconum (=seat of the heralds). While on the left, there are the works of extension of the same Domus Augustana, due to

Domus Augustana, Courtyard

Domus Flavia, Elliptical fountain

Septimius Severus (193-211): some arches of substructio (out of the ground foundations) which characterise the extraordinary view from the Circus Maximus and the Baths of the Emperor and Maxentius (306-312). Worth remembering then is that, next to the crossing between Via di San Gregorio and Via del Circo Massimo, there was an imposing fountain built by Septimius Severus, the Septizonium or Septizodium. What remained was destroyed in order to create a great triumphal street commissioned by Pope Sixtus V, during the visit of Emperor Charles V (1536-1589). Today a row of cypresses reminds us of its proper site.

ISIAC HALL

In the northern corner of the Domus Flavia, below the so-called Basilica, the Isiac Hall has been recently reopened to the public. It is a small apsed room dating from the first years of Augustus' reign (about 20 BC). Initially it was covered by frescoes of the II Style of the Pompeian painting. The frescoes were taken off the walls, and are now shown in the "Loggetta Mattei". They represent episodes connected with the Egyptian divinity Isis, whose cult widely spread in Rome after the conquest of Egypt in 31 BC. The Isiac Hall was discovered in 1724, but then it was covered again, and it was finally brought to light in 1912.

HOUSE OF THE GRIFFONS

The House of the Griffons is situated below the so-called Larario (an altar dedicated to the divinity-protectress of houses) of the Domus Flavia. It is a Republican house, on which the Palace of Domitian was built. It is an interesting place for the magnificent second Style frescoes, now unstuck, which represent the griffons – winged mythological animals with a he-goat head and the body of a lion.

44

PALATINE MUSEUM   The Palatine Museum is situated in the ex-Convent of the Visitazione, restored in 1937. It contains remains dating from the prehistoric age to the end of the 4th century Anno Domini,

with numerous fragments of Greek originals and Roman copies of Skopas' and Prassitele's works. On the ground floor, you will also see the ruins of the Imperial Palace of Domitian (81-96) on which the convent had been built. You will also admire handworks of different ages, from the Palaeolithic (40,000 BC) up to the Republican period (end of the I century BC). The second room houses crockeries and funereal urns dating from the Iron age (9th-8th centuries BC) and also reconstructions of the early Roman huts. In the 4th room there are earthen masks painted in the Republican age. On the first floor, the 5th room contains Augustan pieces dating from the end of the I century BC to the beginning of the I century AD, among which a magnificent Corinthian capital, and three female hermas, in black Egyptian marble, from the temple of Apollo Palatine. The hermas were pillars usually situated at the road crossings to protect the wayfarers. In the 6th room, there are fragments from the Domus Transitoria with very refined marble inlayed tarsias representing stylized or figurative patterns. Monumental sculptures from the Imperial Houses are located in the 9th room. Going out of the Museum, on the left, there is a 16th century public building, the so-called Casino Farnese.

LOGGIA MATTEI   This place belonged to a wide villa built around 1520 by a noble family, on the ruins of the Domus Augustana - the private residence of Domitian. Paolo Mattei bought it in 1561 and added some modifications, his heirs did the same in the next years. After many transfers of the title, in the middle of the 19th century, the villa was incorporated into a convent and, in 1906, it became a State property. The frescoes are now owned by the Metropolitan Museum of New York. They are ascribed to the refined painter and architect from Siena Baldassarre Peruzzi (1481-1536) and his scholars. The Loggia contains paintings from the Isiac Hall.

The majestic arcades visible from Via di San Gregorio are the final part of the extension, built by the Emperor Domitian (81-96) to link his Palace to the aqueduct of Claudius in the middle of the I century AD.

AQUEDUCT OF CLAUDIUS

These baths, built by the Emperor Elagabalus (218-222) not far from the temple of the Sun, are situated on the side facing the Coliseum, along the final part of the Via Sacra.

BATHS OF ELAGABALUS

In 1955, the gate of the 16th century architect Vignola was reassembled here. Originally it was the monumental entrance from the Forum to the so-called Farnesian Horts – the majestic villa built in the middle of the 16th century by Cardinal Alessandro Farnese, Pope Paul III's nephew. In the inferior part, ashlars, pillars and columns were used, while the upper part presents an arched opening, sided by two female hermas (pillars with half-length bust statues). Everywhere you will find the lily, symbol of the Farnese Family.

GATE OF THE FARNESIAN HORTS

Outside the fence of the excavations, in Via di San Bonaventura, there are two small churches. The first, San Sebastiano, is situated near the wide temple built by the Emperor Elagabalus and dedicated to the Egyptian god. It dates from the 10th century, but it was restored in the 17th century. The second church, San Bonaventura, dates from the end of the 17th century.

CHURCHES OF SAN SEBASTIANO AND SAN BONAVENTURA

CIRCUS MAXIMUS As the name says, it was the largest circus in Rome, where biga (two-horse chariot) races took place. At present, it is a garden and some parts have still to be discovered. According to the tradition, it was built during the age of the Etruscan kings (7th c. BC), but it was rebuilt and restored several times, during the Republican and the Imperial periods. It reached its greatest dimension under Emperor Trajan at the beginning of the II century. It was more than 600 m long, almost 200 m wide and could seat about 300,000 spectators. The central reservation, called "spina", around which the bigas raced, was 340 m long and was restored with statues, niches and small sanctuaries. In 10 BC, Augustus decided to erect an obelisk there, carried from Eliopoli. In the middle of the 4th c., Emperor Constance II set up there another obelisk from Tebe. Both the obelisks were taken away in 1587 by Sixtus V and erected respectively in Piazza del Popolo and Piazza San Giovanni. The two long linear sides were as they are today, while only one of the short sides, (that facing Piazza di Porta Capena), was curved. The Imperial box faced the Palatine, while on the straight short side, there were the carceres (gates) which let the chariots go out. The external part presented a prospect with three orders of arcades. Towards the curved side, you will note a medieval building which belonged to the ancient Frangipane's fortress. In Piazzale Romolo e Remo the monument stands, finished in 1949, in honor of one of the most important patriots of the 19th c. Giuseppe Mazzini, who advocated the Unity of Italy. From here, you will admire a fascinating view towards the Palatine with the ruins of the Domus Augustana (exhedra in the centre), of the Palace of Septimius Severus (on the right) and towards the Circus Maximus. The peculiar Baroque façade, on the bottom left, hides a wing of Santa Anastasia's church.

Coliseum

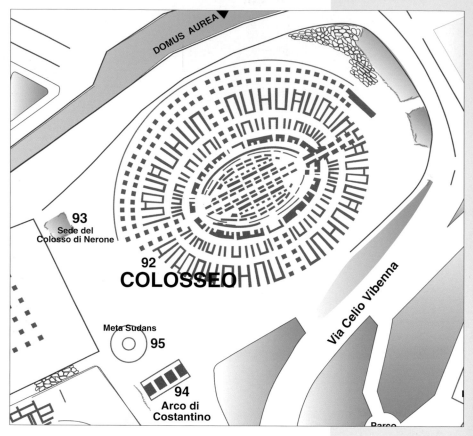

93
Sede del
Colosso di Nerone

92
COLOSSEO

Meta Sudans
95

94
**Arco di
Costantino**

DOMUS AUREA

Via Celio Vibenna

Parco

It is the largest and most famous amphitheatre of the Roman world. It gets its name from a colossal statue of Nero, now disappeared, that was about 32 m high, in golden bronze, which stood in the site today marked by a flowerbed with trees, opposite the exit of the underground station.

The building was begun in 72 AD under the Emperor Vespasian (69-79), who, according to the tradition, wanted to construct a great arena in the same place where his predecessor Nero, unpopular with the Roman probably for the fire he had provoked in 64, had constructed an artificial lake belonging to his luxurious imperial residence, the Domus Aurea. For this reason Vespasian drained the valley that still has an existing channel and raised the ground level about 10 m, reaching the height it has today. Titus (79-81) completed the works of the Coliseum and opened it to the public in 80 AD.

Suetonius (70-140 AD) narrates that "after the inauguration of

the amphitheatre he showed a very organised and colossal event. He presented a naval battle in the old naumachy; (and) here, even gladiators and 5000 wild animals of every kind were killed in one day" (from "The lives of the 12 Caesars – the divine Titus, chapter 7th"). His successor Domitian (81-96) then completed the work, hanging bronze shields on top and perhaps digging underground vaults.

The Coliseum is elliptical in form; its axes measure 188m and 156m. It has a 527m circumference, while the height of the external wall reaches 50m. It could seat up to 50,000 spectators. The external ring made of travertine from Tivoli encloses a cavea, held up by seven pillars and arcades. The arena, that is the scene, with its probable wooden flooring, no longer exists. Below there were the underground vaults, built to accommodate gladiators and wild animals who were brought to the surface by a system of pulleys. Only half of the Coliseum is preserved. In origin it consisted of 80 superimposed columns on three orders, separated by cornices, with statues inside. The numerous and irregular holes visible in the travertine depend on the fact that, during the Middle Ages and the Renaissance, the lead and iron which linked the different blocks were removed. The arcades, on the top of pillars with brackets, are framed by semicolumns of the Tuscan order on the first floor, of Ionic order on the second and Corinthian on the third floor. Then there is an attic with still

Underground areas of the Coliseum

Corinthian pilasters, lightened by windows opening at regular spaces.

This model of successive architectural orders was used in the façades of the Renaissance palaces. It is likely that, according to the tradition, the blind walls were decorated with shields, done by Domitian.

At about two thirds the height of the attic, there was a series of brackets, most of them preserved, on which stood the poles supporting the "velarium", probably a three-gore silk or linen awning which covered the terraces. A group of 100 sailors coming from the port of Misenus, near Pozzuoli raised the awning. The supporting poles passed in the corresponding holes of the high cornice, which closed the building towards the top.

Restoration by architect Stern

The cavea was divided into five horizontal sectors; the first four had marble seats where the men sat, according to their social status; below the senators, then the knights, the plebeians, and in the fifth wooden order, under the colonnade the women sat. The numbered seats, called vomitoria, let the spectators in and out quickly. The galleries and the cross-vaulted corridors were decorated with stuccoes and frescoes. People did not have to pay to watch the shows, because the Emperors let them in free up to the 5th century. No traces of the structures used for the naumachies (=naval battles) have been found. According to some sources, these battles probably took place also during Vespasian's and Domitian's eras.

TIME TRANSFORMATIONS IN THE

COLISEUM

Gladiator duels were forbidden in 438, and in 533, under the reign of Emperor Teodoricus, the shows stopped. The Coliseum then decayed and in the 9th century it was incorporated into the Frangipane's fortress and became a Church property in the middle of the 13th century.

In 1349, an earthquake caused the fall of the side facing the Celian Hill. The amphitheatre then became a marble quarry and its blocks were taken for the construction of numerous Roman palaces of the Renaissance and Baroque periods, such as those of Farnese, Barberini and of the Cancelleria.

Sixtus V (1585-90) then turned it into a woollen factory, while Pope Benedict XIV (1740-58) consecrated the arena to the memory of the Christians, who were never killed there.

Pope Pius VII (1800-23), after the strong earthquake of 1806, decided to have it restored by the architect Raffaele Stern. He planned and built the eastern buttress and the brick walls which had to "block" the falling arcades, as to stop time. In the plugging wall he used bricks in contrast with the original travertine. We do not know if he did it to distinguish the original from the restored parts or simply to economise on costs.

The works continued on the front side, facing Via dei Fori Imperiali under Leon XII (1823-29) and they were directed by Giuseppe Valadier, author of the famous buttress.

He used the same technique of his predecessor and the fame of his work dimmed Stern's. The brick arcades are in a decreasing order from the bottom. The works were completed in 1826 with the epigraph and the date. The restoration of the Coliseum finished under Pope Pius IX, when the architect Canina completed the inner circle of the west-side arcades from 1846 to 1852. Presently the great monument is being restored in order to consolidate the structures and to clean the wide travertine surfaces, blackened by deposits of polluting materials, which have created the so-called "black crust".

The arch was situated along the triumphal way, where the victorious armies marched. It has three arcades, and it is 25 m high. According to the tradition, it was built by Emperor Constantine to celebrate his victory over Maxentius at the Milvian Bridge in 312, after which he granted freedom of worship to the Christians with the Edict of Milan in 313. Recent studies and minute examinations have however revealed the existence of a previous structure, from the base to the border, built during the age of Trajan (98-117) or Hadrian (117-138). Constantine is said to have re-used the above said structure, adding the attic with the inscription and the spolia reliefs, dating from the II century. From a stylistic point of view, the sculptures dating from Trajan's and Hadrian's ages, seen above all in the tondos, are elegant, well-proportioned and harmonious with the surroundings. Those dating from Antoninus Pius' (138-161) and Marcus Aurelius' times are characterised by a gradual reduction of depth, with figures tending to occupy all the available space. Under Constantine, instead, the bodies are completely out of proportion, with big heads and out of scale architectonic elements. This is particularly evident in the slab where the Emperor sits in the centre. He rises over his subjects and his court dignitaries are crowded in a fence; the distortion of the image is part of architecture now and only in the 13th century in Italian art, did an essential recovery in volume and form begin again.

ARCH OF CONSTANTINE

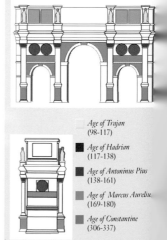

Age of Trajan
(98-117)

Age of Hadrian
(117-138)

Age of Antoninus Pius
(138-161)

Age of Marcus Aurelius
(169-180)

Age of Constantine
(306-337)

Arch of Constantine and traces of the Meta Sudans

META SUDANS   The name derives from Latin (méta = a cone-shaped figure and sudans = jetting). It was a big Roman fountain dating from the end of the I century BC, truncated cone-shaped, 18 m high and 16m large at its base, situated between the Coliseum and the Arch of Constantine. Still visible in the old photos, it was demolished in 1936 to pave the area linking Via dei Fori Imperiali and the Passeggiata Archeologica.

Recent excavations of the Soprintendenza have discovered its foundations.

DOMUS AUREA

T he remains of the Domus Aurea belong only in part to the extraordinary residence built by the Emperor Nero (54-68 AD), a year after the fire of 64, which destroyed a great part of Rome in nine days. The Domus Aurea is made up of a series of pavilions surrounded by a big park; it extended from the Palatine to the Celian and Oppian hills , and probably even to the Esquilin. Inside, it contained the depression, now occupied by the Coliseum, where an artificial small lake had been constructed. The enormous complex was adorned with statues from Greece and with monumental fountains. The Latin historian Suetonius (70-140) gives us a famous description of it in his work on the Emperors' lives: "There was nothing however in which he was more ruinously prodigal than in building. He made a palace extending all the way from the Palatine to the Esquiline, which at first he called the House of Passage, but when it was burned shortly after its completion and rebuilt, the Golden House. Its size and splendour will be sufficiently indicated by the following details. Its vestibule was large enough to contain a colossal statue of the emperor a hundred and twenty feet high; and it was so extensive that it had a triple colonnade a mile long. There was a pond too, like a sea, surrounded with buildings to represent cities, besides tracts of country, varied by tilled fields, vineyards, pastures and woods, with great numbers of wild and domestic animals. In the rest of the house all parts were overlaid with gold and adorned with gems and mother-of-pearl. There were dining rooms with fretted ceilings of ivory, whose panels could turn and shower down flowers and were fitted with pipes for sprinkling the guests with perfumes. The main banquet hall was circular and constantly revolved day and night, like the heavens. He had baths supplied with sea water and sulphur water. When the edifice was finished in this style and he dedicated it, he designed to say nothing more in the way of approval than that he was at last beginning to be housed like a human being. (The test by Suetonius, The lives of the Caesars, b.VI, chap. XXXI is translated by S.C. Rolfe, edited by Loeb Classical Library). The historical sources handed down also the names of the artists who worked there, the architects Severus and Celere, and the painter Fabullo, famous only for his pictures in the Domus.

Today, only a few traces of this huge complex are still visible on the Palatine and Celian Hills and in the area of the Imperial Fora. They were built using pre-existing masonries. Most of its remains are on the Oppian Hill. It is well preserved thanks to the filling of the ground and the following constructions which also used the walls as foundations, because Titus (79-81) and Trajan (98-117) wanted to erase the memory of their predecessor.

Dug in the '30s and in the first years of the '50s, after 20 years of restoration, the Domus Aurea was partially re-opened to the public in June 1999, 32 out of 140 original rooms of the pavilion can now be visited and soon, other

Cup with serpent-like handles

Statue of the Muse Tersicore

Octagonal Hall

places, still in the digging phase, will be open.

To understand the real architecture of the great Neronian residence, you should, first of all, imagine it without the Trajanian oblique walls, windowed southwards, where the main rooms are situated, completely sunlit. An irregular semi-octagonal courtyard was the centre of the two asymmetric wings of the main pavilion, about 240m long. The rooms, all barrel-vaulted, were from 10 to 11m high. Traces of the holes for the false ceiling made of reeds, which lowered their height, still remain. Among the most famous rooms, there is the golden vaulted Hall, in axis with the central courtyard and the octagonal Hall, a real masterpiece of Roman architecture. Probably Suetonius refers to this one in the above said work, even if no traces of the rotating mechanisms have been found. In this last architectonic area you will be affected by the slightly lowered vault, made in concrete, and by the magnificent almost squared openings, which have to be considered technically very brave from an architectonic point of view, because of the length of the horizontal element (almost 6m). Even today, it is very difficult to carry out that, without the use of reinforced concrete. From the octagonal Hall, the space widens in the adjacent rooms; worth of interest are the halls on the north side, with a Greek cross plan, next to the nymphaeum.

Dome of the Octagonal Hall

Decorations in the hall of Achille e Sciro

In 69, Nero committed suicide at only 30 years old, and after that, the Domus Aurea was inhabited by the second of the three emperors, who succeeded him in only one year.

At the end of 69, the Empire was ruled by the first of the Flavian family - Vespasian (69-79).

The Celian was not demolished but, after being spoiled of all its precious works of art, was filled with earth thrown from the openings of the vaults. So it became the base of the baths, built later on by Emperor Trajan.

On the site of the antique pond, the Coliseum was erected, also to give back to the Romans the fields previously expropriated.

Forgotten for centuries, it was only in the first years of the 16th century, that the remains of the Domus Aurea were discovered by those artists - such as Raphael - who let themselves down from the top through the openings of the vaults. They thought they were inside caves.

Enthusiastic about the beauty of the paintings found, representing landscapes and refined designs, these artists drew inspiration for a new pictorial trend, called "grotesque". Among the statues found in the Neronian residence, there was the famous Laocoon, a Roman marble copy of an Hellenistic original; discovered in 1505 or 1506, it was greatly admired by Michelangelo.

IMPERIAL FORA

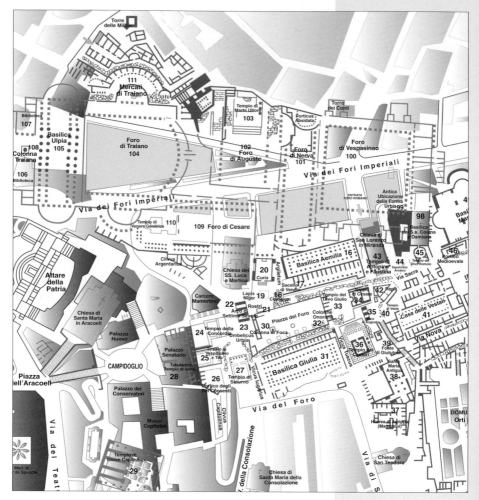

T he "Imperial fora" of ancient Rome were made up of a series of big squares, public buildings, temples and commemorative monuments. Inside and in the more ancient "Roman Forum", the most important public, judicial, religious and civil functions during the Empire were held.

The Imperial Fora were built by Julius Caesar and his successor emperors from 46 BC to the beginning of the II century AD so as to be orthogonally adjacent one to the other to form a unitarian urban complex.

Today, unfortunately such a structure is no longer completely seen for the presence here of Via dei Fori Imperiali, which interrupts its continuity.

Boards with the Roman expansion

VIA DEI FORI IMPERIALI Both the Republican Forum and the Imperial Fora, deserted for centuries (see page 35), became an object of rediscovery and excavations in the middle of 19th c. and then at the end of that century. Only at the beginning of our century many of the ruins visible today were discovered. Via dei Fori Imperiali (at the beginning Via dell'Impero), planned in 1925 by Mussolini, was opened in 1932. It was conceived for antihistorical reasons of monumentality and as an imponent scene for the parades; this street, 850 m long, covered the remains of a whole quarter stratified during the Middle Ages and the Renaissance with a thick layer of bitumen. Indeed it broke what remained of the ancient unity of the forum. Everything was made in a hurry: a lot of findings were destroyed and nobody thought to take pictures or to prove scientifically the findings and the sites.

The four panels situated on the external wall of the basilica of Maxentius date back to this last phase, too. They represent different phases of the expansion of Rome, since its foundation under Trajan (97-117 AD) during whose reign the Empire reached its maximum expansion.

Today the trend is to reduce the wideness of this big and now important street in Rome, trying to recreate the unity of the Fora, as far as possible. The greatest archaeological site in the world would thus be created: from Piazza Venezia to Via Appia. This fascinating plan will require a very long time to be done, as it is difficult to find an alternative to the heavy traffic passing along this way. For this reason excavations are being held in that area, which was used as a garden until some times ago.

The Forum of Julius Caesar , the first of the Imperial Fora, was planned by the conqueror of the Gauls to widen the existing public spaces, not enough for the million of Romans who lived in Rome at that time.

The Forum was inaugurated in 46 BC and it consisted of a rectangular square with a portico. A temple faced one of the shorter sides, superimposed on a podium with front entrance stairways, pronaos and unique cella, dedicated to the goddess Venus. Caesar in fact claimed to descend from her, through her son Aeneas.

Only the left corner and part of the basement of the Temple with three columns still exist. The brick shaft has been restored of course, while the bronze statue representing the Emperor is a copy.

FORUM OF AUGUSTUS

Temple of Augustus, detail

According to the ancient texts, the first Emperor of Rome, Augustus (27 BC - 14 AD), inaugurated his Forum in 2 AD. What remains of this structure is on the same side of the Imperial buildings.

It was perpendicular to the Forum of Caesar, and it consisted of a rectangular square with a portico, with the short side facing east enclosed by a temple. This temple is bigger than Venus' one, but it has the same characteristics. Augustus dedicated it both to Mars Ultor (the Avenger) to commemorate his own victory on Caesar's murderers, and to the goddess Venus, considered by the Emperor his progenitrix. The square was enclosed on both sides by two exhedras with statues of Aeneas and Romulus, who, according to the tradition, were the founders of the Romans. On the back of the temple (see the line of the roof) a peperine wall divided the complex from the Suburra, a famous popular district of ancient Rome, characterised by wood buildings which frequently burst into flames. A quadriga with the statue of Augustus stood opposite the temple.

63

The next forum built by Emperor Vespasian (69-79 AD) has completely disappeared. Its ruins are buried at the junction between Via dei Fori Imperiali and Via Cavour. It contained the so-called great temple of Peace, which showed the relics of the war led by Vespasian's son - Titus (79-81) against the Jews in Palestine.

A few things remain of the forum built by Domitian (91-96) and completed by Nerva (96-98). It was very long and rectangular in shape, and tied up the three previous squares in order to connect them. For this reason the Forum was also known as Transitorium. The Forum was crossed by the street Argiletum, which linked it to the Republican Forum and the Suburra district. It was dominated by the Temple dedicated to Minerva. In the Renaissance pictures, some parts of the Forum were still visible, but now only two columns of the lateral wall enclosing the Forum stand. They are superimposed by a frieze with female work scenes and by a statue of the goddess Minerva, protector of handcraft.

In the plan to refurbish the Forum, the great sewer of the 17th century - built on the Roman and Medieval buildings - will be used to link the two dug areas of the Fora, now separated by Via dei Fori Imperiali.

FORUM OF TRAJAN
The Forum of Trajan (98-117) was the last and the richest forum. The entrance is from the Markets side. Probably built by Apollodorus of Damascus, one of the greatest architects of the time, it consisted of a series of buildings and spaces. These were: 1) A big square with a portico with two side exhedras, and, in the middle, an equestrian monument - no longer existing - dedicated to him; 2) the so-called Basilica Ulpia (from Ulpis, the name of the emperor) with its five aisles and two lateral apses; 3) two libraries, Greek and Latin, enclosing a small space - in the centre stood the spiral column (with external decoration) representing the Trajanian wars in Dacia (now Romania); 4) an enclosure beyond which there was perhaps a temple dedicated to Divus Trajan, built by his successor Hadrian (117-138). Recent excavations let us suppose that this last monument was on the opposite side, towards the square with the portico, thus linked to the Forum of Augustus. At the slope of

the Quirinal Hill, the Markets completed this majestic complex.

The well-preserved Column follows the Roman volumen (a parchment scroll rolled up on a pole); it was probably situated between the two libraries to be better "read". The Column stood on a base containing the burial urns of the Emperor and his wife. It was made up of dry-stone blocks of marble one on the top of the other, without mortar; it was 100 Roman foot high (29.60 m from the base up to the Corinthian capital).

On the top of the column the statue of Trajan was placed, but in 1585, Sixtus V replaced it with the statue of Saint Peter with keys in his hand, watching the basilica being built dedicated to him.

The spirit of the time tended to "christianise" the pagan buildings.

The frieze, higher on the top, so as to have a better view from the bottom, represents the two wars led by the Emperor in Dacia (the first in 101-2, the second in 105-7) in more than 2,500 figures.

At the 12th circle the two

Trajanian Column

cycles are divided by a famous winged Victory, copied in the Middle Ages and Renaissance. Reasonably, some experts think that the column was coloured; in the past it was surely whitewashed, that is, covered externally by a thin layer of milk of lime which has helped its preservation over time.

MARKETS OF TRAJAN   On the slope of the Quirinal, facing the Forum, there was the extraordinary complex of the Markets. There were six levels of streets with some tabernae (= shops) and warehouses. We do not know the origin of time of the building, generally attributed to Trajan, but it was probably started by Domitian (86-96). Apollodorus of Damascus is supposed to be the architect, the same of the Forum of Trajan. This fragment of Imperial Rome strikes for the integrity of the still visible structure of the city, despite the restorations and the missing parts. It lets us imagine a complex and well-built city, strangely "modern" and present.

The archaeologist Corrado Ricci (1926-34) discovered and did the first restoration works. During the medieval time, on the ruins of the Markets, the Militia Tower was built – it was the Palace of the Knights of Rhodes, seat of the Order of Malta, in the 15th century.

CHURCHES IN THE FORUM

The churches of Santa Francesca Romana and Sts Cosmas and Damian are situated beside the remains of the magnificent walls of the Basilica of Maxentius and are built on ancient ruins.

Santa Francesca Romana stands in part on the ancient temple of Venus (II c. AD). It was built in the High Middle Ages, and was reconstructed in the 10th century with the name of Santa Maria Nova. It was then restored in the 12th century – the same period the bell tower dates back to – and again adapted in the 13th century. In 1440, the church was dedicated to Santa Francesca Romana, founder of the order of the Oblates, after the burial of her body in the crypt beneath. It was restored again during the Baroque period; the white travertine façade was completed in 1615.

Inside, in the apsidal conch and over the altar, there are images of the Virgin dating back to the 12th century, while in the sacristy you will find a rare example of painting on wood, dating from 6th or 7th century.

Santa Francesca Romana is the protector of car drivers, so each year, on 9th March, a lot of believers drive their cars near the church to have them blessed.

CHURCH OF SANTA FRANCESCA ROMANA

CHURCH OF SAINTS COSMAS AND DAMIAN

The Basilica is dedicated to Sts Cosmas and Damian - two Syrian doctors, perhaps martyred under Diocletian (284-305).

It was built in 527 by Pope Felix IV (526-530) in an area of the Forum of Vespasian, and it was altered in the first half of the 17th century. Here you will see several rare witnesses of medieval art in Rome. On the triumphal arch, there are mosaic decorations dating from the 6th century, representing Christ in the middle of a road, made of red and blue clouds. Red is the colour of fire, so it refers to Hell; blue is the colour of air and Eden. Christ is surrounded by the saints Peter, Paul, Cosmas and Damian, Theodore and also Pope Felix IV – a figure completely rebuilt in 1660 –with the church model in his hand. Below is the river Jordan, with 12 sheep in front of Christ, representing the 12 apostles. All these decorations were altered during the Baroque restorations. In the Chapel, facing the entrance, there is a rare fresco of the 8th century, showing Christ crucifix dressed in Byzantine style. Not to be missed then is the splendid 18th century Neapolitan Crib (entrance from Via dei Fori Imperiali).

On the external façade, that belonged to a room of the Forum of Vespasian, there was the Forma Urbis. It was the plan of Rome engraved on 151 slabs of stone, dated 203-211. 146 pieces have been found and they are now preserved in the Museum of Palazzo Braschi.

ROMAN EMPERORS AND THEIR WORKS IN ROME

Forum of Caesar

Theatre of Marcellus

Forum of Augustus

Domus Aurea

THE JULIO CLAUDIAN EMPERORS:

AUGUSTUS *27 BC-14 AD: first emperor of Rome, completed the forum of Caesar and added one more square with a Temple dedicated to himself. He built the first Pantheon, Baths and Theatres in Rome.*

TIBERIUS *14-37 AD: Built the Imperial Palace on the Palatine Hill.*

CALIGULA *37-41: Began the aqueduct named after himself, still visible on the Via Appia.*

CLAUDIUS *41-54: Built an inlay in the mouth of the river Tiber, so starting the first core of Porto and enlarged the Imperial Palaces, completed the aqueduct.*

NERO *54-68: Built the Domus Aurea and a great Circus on the Vatican Hill.*

THE FLAVIANS:

VESPASIAN *69-79: Built his own forum, no longer existing, and began the Temple of Peace and the Coliseum.*

TITUS *79-81: Completed and inaugurated the Coliseum.*

DOMITIAN *81-96: Completed the Coliseum with decorations and the underground excavations; he built the arch dedicated to his father Titus and the stadium of Ancus Marcius (then Piazza Navona).*

Coliseum

Arch of Titus

NERVA *96-98: Built his forum between those of Augustus and Vespasian.*

TRAJAN *98-117: Built a majestic forum containing a basilica, two libraries, the spiral column and the famous markets; the architect was Apollodorus of Damascus. He made an exagonal port at the mouth of the Tiber.*

HADRIAN *117-138: Commissioned the Pantheon, Villa Adriana at Tivoli and his own Mausoleum, he restored Ostia.*

Forum of Trajan

Pantheon

THE ANTONINES:

ANTONINUS PIUS *138-161: Adorned the Roman forum with the temple of Venus and the Temple of Antoninus and Faustina.*

MARCUS AURELIUS *161-180: Built the Aurelian Column, his statue stands on the Capitol.*

COMMODUS *180-192: the reliefs on the Arch of Constantine belong to him*

Temple of Antoninus and Faustina

Statue of Marcus Aurelius

THE SEVERANS:

SEPTIMIUS SEVERUS *193-211: Restored the palaces on the Palatine, built the Septizonium and the Arch dedicated to himself. He started the Baths of Caracalla.*

CARACALLA *211-217: Completed the famous Baths.*

ELAGABALUS *218-222: On the Palatine he built the baths and the Temple dedicated to the Sun.*

ALEXANDER SEVERUS *222-235: Rebuilt the scene of the Theatre of Marcellus*

Arch of Septimius Severus

AURELIAN *270-275: Built the round walls.*

DIOCLETIAN *284-305: Built the famous Baths.*

MAXENTIUS *306-312: Started the great basilica in the Roman Forum and built the Circus on the Via Appia.*

CONSTANTINE *306-337: Completed the Basilica of Maxentius*

576: Fall of the Western Roman Empire.

Basilica of Maxentius

GLOSSARY

FRESCO: painting executed on wet plaster.

ASHLAR: masonry uniformly projecting from the wall.

RUSTIC ASHLAR: ashlar, often with a tough surface finish.

CARDO: in the Roman town, it refers to one of the two main streets, directed North-South.

CELLA: in the Greek or Roman temples, it was a space with statues of divinities in, forbidden to prayers.

SPIRAL COLUMN: a majestic column with spiral internal stairs.

DECUMANUS: in the Roman town, it was the second street, perpendicular to the cardo, directed East-West.

DOMUS: patrician Roman house, characterised by one or two courtyards, overlooked by the rooms.

ENTABLATURE: a horizontal architectonic element above a column. It is made up of three parts: architrave, frieze and cornice.

HERM: pillar or semipillar, decreased in girth towards the base, surmonted by a human bust.

HORREA: warehouses for food stockage.

INSULA: more storey-house, with shops on the street level.

NYMPHAEUM: monumental fountain.

ORDER OF ARCHITECTURE: In architecture it refers to the column (base, shaft and capital) and its entablature (architrave, frieze and cornice). According to the historians of the Renaissance, there were five orders:

DORIC: developed in the 7th century BC in the Greek region of Peloponneso and Magna Grecia; the column was fluted and without a base; the capital had a flat abacus (upper part) resting on the echinus (lower); above it, the entablature was made up of a flat architrave, a frieze with grooved elements (triglyphs) and carved slabs (metopes); a cornice completed it.
IONIC: developed in Asia Minor and in the Attic region since the 6th c. BC; the Romans made a great use of it. The column with a base was taller and slenderer; the capital had symmetrical volutes; the entablature had a three-levelled architrave and a frieze showing a continuous relief.
CORINTHIAN: Greek in origin (5th century BC), the Romans developed it; similar to the Ionic order as far as regards the column and its entablature, the capital had acanthus leaves.
TUSCAN: used by the Etruscans since the 6th century BC and by the Romans, it simplified the Doric order - the column was not fluted and had a base.
COMPOSITE: used by the Romans since the end of the I century AD; the capital had Ionic volutes (in the upper part) and acanthus leaves in the lower part. The entablature is similar to that in the Corinthian order.

| DORIC | IONIC | CORINTHIAN | TUSCAN | COMPOSITE |

PARASTA: a structural flat pilaster, engaged in a wall and projecting only slightly from it.

PILASTER: a decorative semicolumn, engaged in a wall and projecting only slightly from it.

PRONAOS: in the Greek and Roman temples, it referred to an open space in front of the cella; sometimes it was enclosed by side walls.

PROTYROS: architectonic element with columns, arch and tympanum, showing the front entrance to a house or a church.

SUBSTRUCTIO: out of the ground foundation wall.

TABERNAE: shops, also for handcraft activities.

BUILDING TECHNIQUES

OPUS QUADRATUM : masonry of large tufa or stone parallelepipedal blocks.
The blocks often measured a multiple of the Roman foot (29,6 cm). In the Archaic age (8th-7th c. BC) they were just superimposed - that is without mortar, bearing their own weight ; later on, the blocks were held by iron or bronze cramps, with very little binder.

OPUS CAEMENTICIUM : mixture of : a) lime (crushed calcareous stone), b) sand or pozzolana (volcanic earth), c) pieces of stone, bricks, marble or travertine. All was mixed with water and poured in wooden formworks.
Once solid, the formwork was taken away. It was very resistant and was largely used since the III c. BC in the internal walls, so as to have curved lines in plans or in vaults or domes. In different ages, the opus was covered in different ways, as illustrated here below.

OPUS INCERTUM : the most ancient covering of the opus caementicium. It is made up of pyramidal tufa blocks, with irregular base, set in the mortar, showing the largest part. The wall was then plastered. It was used from the II c. BC to the I c. AD.

OPUS QUASI RETICOLATUM : small tufa blocks set in quite regular rows, even if not perfectly organised. Used from the end of the II c. BC and the beginning of the I c. AD.

OPUS RETICOLATUM : covering made of pyramidal tufa blocks with square bases: the top is set in the mortar, while the base is external, thus making a characteristic network pattern with oblique lines at 45°. The edges were made of superimposed rectangular tufa blocks, the wall was then plastered. Used from the first half of the I c. AD to the end of the I c. AD, when it was gradually replaced by the opus mixtum.

OPUS LATERICIUM : from lateres = tiles or sun-baked bricks: pressed and flattened clay with or without straw, sun-baked (mattone crudo). Used by people in Mesopotamia, it was then used by the Romans from the II c. BC to the age of Augustus (beginning I c. AD), when the kiln-baked brick was introduced.

OPUS TESTACEUM or testacea structura: covering of the opus caementicium made of baked bricks; triangle shaped, the bricks had the vertex in the mortar and the hypotenuse is external. Sometimes these walls were left in sight, as in modern times; other times they presented regular holes in which were driven the cramps of the marble covering. Rarely were they plastered. Used during the age of Augustus (beginning of I c. AD), it was gradually replaced by the opus vittatum.

OPUS MIXTUM : covering of the opus caementicium, made of the opus reticolatum and the opus latericium. This masonry was used in the edges, so as to strengthen the side wall and contrasting the possible cracks along the oblique lines. Very used during the Flavians (from 70 AD), under Trajan (98-117) and Hadrian (117-138). The wall was then plastered.

OPUS LISTATUM or VITTATUM, from vitta =bend. Covering of the opus caementicium formed by alternate horizontal rows of bricks and parallelepipedal small blocks of tufa; sometimes there are two rows of bricks and one of tufa. This opus was very regular and was used since Antoninus Pius (138-161); it became predominating since the 4th c. AD, above all under Emperors Maxentius (306-12) and Constantine (306-337), probably due to the poor production of bricks. The wall was then plastered.

BRICKSTAMPS : factory marks on tiles or bricks. Often, when the brick has not been re-used, it can date the building. Used from the I century BC to the age of Caracalla (198-217).

| OPUS QUADRATUM | OPUS RETICULATUM | OPUS TESTACEUM | OPUS MIXTUM | OPUS VITTATUM |

PLAN OF THE FORUM BOARIUM AND THE PALATINE

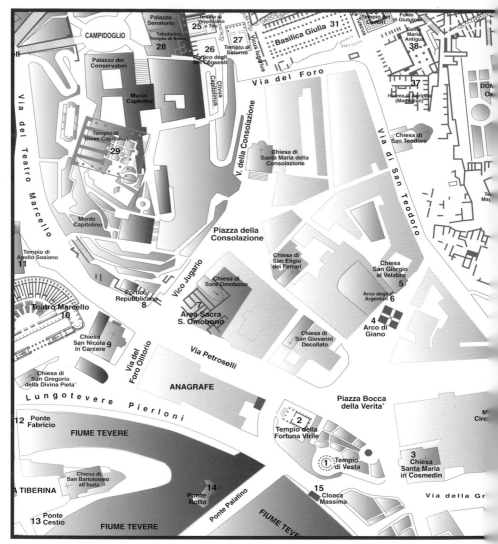

FORUM BOARIUM
1. TEMPLE OF VESTA
2. TEMPLE OF FORTUNA VIRILIS
3. CHURCH OF SANTA MARIA IN COSMEDIN
4. ARCH OF JANUS
5. CHURCH OF SAN GIORGIO IN VELABRO
6. ARCH OF THE ARGENTARI
7. ARCHEOLOGICAL SITE OF S. OMOBONO
8. REPUBLICAN PORTICO
9. CHURCH OF SAN NICOLA IN CARCERE
10. THEATRE OF MARCELLUS
11. TEMPLE OF APOLLO SOSIANUS
12. FABRICIO BRIDGE
13. CESTIO BRIDGE
14. ROTTO BRIGDE
15. CLOACA MAXIMA

THE PALATINE
53. FARNESE AVIARY
54. ROMULUS' HUTS
55. TEMPLE OF MAGNA MATER
56. STAIRS OF CACUS
57. ARCHAIC CISTERNS
58. HOUSE OF LIVIA
59. HOUSE OF AUGUSTO
60. TEMPLE OF APOLLO
61. DOMUS TIBERIANA
62. CRYPTOPORTICO OF NERO
63. PALACE OF DOMITIAN
64. DOMUS FLAVIA

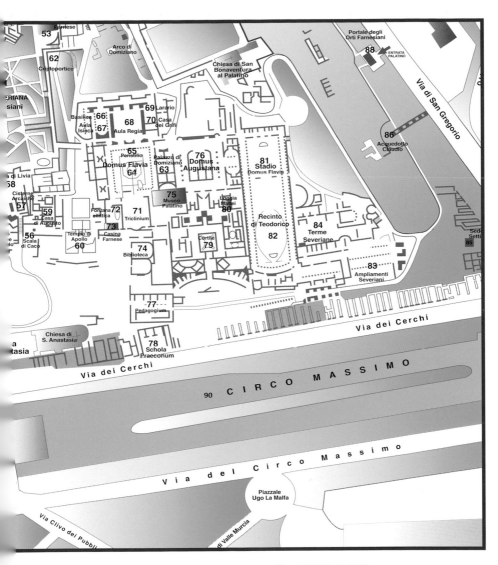

65.	PERISTILIUM	80.	LOGGIA MATTEI
66.	BASILICA	81.	STADIUM
67.	ISIAC HALL	82.	THEODORIC'S ENCLOSURE
68.	REGIA HALL	83.	SEVERIAN ENLARGMENTS
69.	LARARIO	84.	SEVERIAN BATHS
70.	HOUSE OF THE GRIFFONS	85.	SEPTIZONIUM
71.	TRICLINIUM	86.	AQUEDUCT OF CLAUDIUS
72.	ELLIPTICAL FOUNTAIN	87.	BATHS OF ELAGABALUS
73.	FARNESIAN HOUSE	88.	GATE OF THE FARNESIAN HORTS
74.	LIBRARY	89.	TEMPLE OF THE SUN
75.	PALATINE MUSEUM	90.	CIRCUS MAXIMUS
76.	DOMUS AUGUSTANA	91.	MITREO OF THE CIRCUS MAXIMUS
77.	PEDAGOGIUM		
78.	SCHOLA PRAECONUM		
79.	COURTYARD		

Plan of the Roman Forum and the Imperial Fora

ROMAN FORUM

16.	BASILICA AEMILIA	31.	BASILICA JULIA
17.	SACELLO OF VENUS	32.	COLUMNS
18.	COMITIUM	33.	TEMPLE OF DIVUS JULIUS
19.	LAPIS NIGER	34.	ALTAR OF CAESAR
20.	CURIA	35.	ARCH OF AUGUSTUS
21.	ARCH OF JANUS	36.	TEMPLE OF THE CASTORS
22.	ARCH OF SEPTIMIUS SEVERUS	37.	HORREA OF AGRIPPA
23.	UMBELICUS URBIS	38.	CHURCH OF SANTA MARIA ANTIQUA
24.	TEMPLE OF THE CONCORDIA	39.	FOUNTAIN OF JUTURNA
25.	TEMPLE OF VESPASIAN AND TITUS	40.	TEMPLE OF VESTA
26.	PORTICO OF THE DEI CONSENTI	41.	HOUSE OF THE VESTALS
27.	TEMPLE OF SATURN	42.	REGIA
28.	TABULARIUM	43.	TEMPLE OF ANTONINUS AND FAUSTINA
29.	TEMPLE OF JUPITER CAPITOLINUS	44.	ARCHAIC BURIAL GROUND
30.	COLUMN OF PHOCAS	45.	TEMPLE OF DIVUS ROMULUS
		46.	MEDIEVAL PORTICO

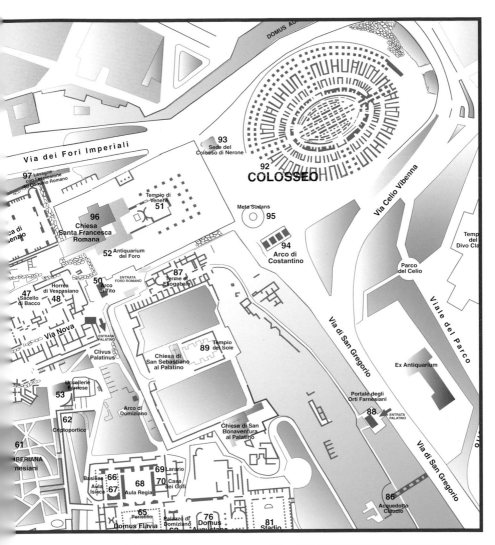

47. SACELLO OF BACCHUS	98. CHURCH OF STS COSMAS AND DAMIAN
48. HORREA OF VESPASIAN	99. ANCIENT LOCATION OF FORMA URBIS
49. BASILICA OF MAXENTIUS	100. FORUM OF VESPASIAN
50. ARCH OF TITUS	101. FORUM OF NERVA
51. TEMPLE OF VENUS	102. FORUM OF AUGUSTUS
52. ANTIQUARIUM OF THE FORUM	103. TEMPLE OF MARS ULTOR
	104. FORUM OF TRAJAN
92. COLISEUM	105. BASILICA ULPIA
93. SEAT OF NERO'S COLOSSUS	106. LIBRARY
94. ARCH OF CONSTANTINE	107. LIBRARY
95. META SUDANS	108. TRAJANIAN COLUMN
	109. FORUM OF CAESAR
	110. TEMPLE OF VENUS GENITRIX
	111. MARKETS OF TRAJAN

IMPERIAL FORA
96. CHURCH OF SANTA FRANCESCA ROMANA
97. BOARDS WITH THE
EXPLOSION OF THE ROMAN DOMINION

INDEX

© Copyright 2000
Ats Italia Editrice srl
This volume was edited by:
ATS Italia Editrice - Rome
Via Francesco Sivori, 6 - tel. and fax 0639726079-0639726080
www.atsitaliaeditrice.it

Author
Sonia Gallico
Editing and Technical Coordination
Frida Giannini
Graphic Project
Ats Italia Editrice (Sabrina Moroni)
Cartographies
Ats Italia Editrice (Sabrina Moroni)
Photolitography
Scriba - Florence
Printing
Papergraf - Padua
Photographs
Archives Ats Italia Editrice (Amantini, Bocchieri, Borchi, Borra,
Cirilli, Cozzi, Giordano, Grassi, Marinelli, Tini)
Translation
Tiziana Vallocchia

ISBN 88-87654-20-4

The editor is available for those having rights on   the unfound iconographical sources